C0-ALQ-503

VINTAGE AUTOMOBILE RACING

George D. Lepp

Motorbooks International
Publishers & Wholesalers
®

First published in 1990 by Motorbooks International Publishers & Wholesalers, P O Box 2, 729 Prospect Avenue, Osceola, WI 54020 USA

© George D. Lepp, 1990

All rights reserved. With the exception of quoting brief passages for the purposes of review no part of this publication may be reproduced without prior written permission from the publisher

Motorbooks International is a certified trademark, registered with the United States Patent Office

The information in this book is true and complete to the best of our knowledge. All recommendations are made without any guarantee on the part of the author or publisher, who also disclaim any liability incurred in connection with the use of this data or specific details

We recognize that some words, model names and designations, for example, mentioned herein are the property of the trademark holder. We use them for identification purposes only. This is not an official publication

Motorbooks International books are also available at discounts in bulk quantity for industrial or sales-promotional use. For details write to Special Sales Manager at the Publisher's address

Library of Congress Cataloging-in-Publication Data
Lepp, George D.
    Vintage automobile racing / George D. Lepp.
        p. cm.
    Includes bibliographical references (p.).
    ISBN 0-87938-422-0
    1. Automobile racing—History—Pictorial works. 2. Automobiles, Racing—History—Pictorial works. 3. Sports car events—History—Pictorial works. 4. Automobiles—Conservation and restoration—Pictorial works. I. Title.
GV1029.15.L47 1990   90-37083
796.7'2'0222—dc20   CIP

Printed and bound in Hong Kong

Contents

The Spirit of Vintage Racing

From the first days of the automobile in the 1900s we just had to race.

And we still do. A dedicated group of vintage automobile racing enthusiasts has continued to run their historic and vintage cars in anger, racing around tracks so that those of us who care can continue to see and hear an important part of our history.

Vintage racers in the United States are a loose-knit group of people. No less than forty organizations and sanctioning bodies are involved in the sport. No one group oversees them all, and that adds variety and flavor to the spectacle. Even the interpretation of what constitutes a vintage or historical racing automobile differs from group to group. Some events are by invitation only with strict adherence to set rules; others are open to anyone with an interest and the required safety equipment. That's how you might find a three-wheel Morgan and a Porsche 911 competing on the track at the same time.

Vintage Production Sports Cars, with one small Formula car behind the Alfa Romeo, come down the esses between Turns 4 and 5 at Georgia's Road Atlanta racetrack. These are the cars from the 1960s that most of us remember well. We either owned a street version, saw them on a daily basis, or still see some of them race in today's SCCA events. The lead car is a 1961 Porsche 356 1600 cc driven by Ron Green, with a smattering of Alfa Romeo GTAs, Lotus Formula cars, Minis and others bringing up the rear.

Vintage racing can be appreciated from several perspectives. At one level it presents a living, moving, sensory museum. Racing cars that have an illustrious past are once again fired up to be seen and heard at speed. Drivers that created marque legends, and who are legends in their own right, are often re-united with their former steeds. Together, they re-create a milieu that few of us experienced firsthand.

Why do we care? It's not that they're all works of visual art in their own rights—they're not. And it's not just the role sports racing has played in developing the advancements of typical street vehicles, such as now-commonplace features like disc brakes, improved suspensions and new styles of tires. It's the combination of the skills of the drivers, the thunder and scream of the red-lined engines, the dust, the danger and the crowds that excites all our senses at once.

The drivers and owners of these rolling museum pieces appreciate the past as few people do—they experience the automobile from the driver's seat. To sit where Juan Manuel Fangio, Jim Clark or Stirling Moss once sat, to squint through that same windscreen—maybe even on the same track—is the ultimate encounter for a vintage racing enthusiast.

The experience doesn't come cheap. The price of historical racing machinery is escalating to astronomical heights.

Another group of owners and drivers that come to vintage racing, however, brings cars that may not be worth hundreds of thousands of dollars nor have acclaimed racing histories. But MGs, Austin-Healey Sprites, Alfa Romeos and the like are significant to vintage racing. To many enthusiasts they offer the chance to get on the track in an affordable vehicle and under conditions less demanding than SCCA club racing. They gather in the paddock in groups, repair in groups and race together as friends.

Owners who believe that these rare automobiles should be seen and heard—instead of locked away safely in storage to appreciate in value, or protected behind ropes in a museum—are the people that enable the next level of participation in vintage racing. They give the spectators the chance to play their own roles in the re-creation of the past. In many cases the cars that participate in vintage racing events are in better condition than the day they first raced. Spectators can walk through the paddock, talk to the owners and actually touch the cars—carefully, please. Vintage race car owners worth their entry fees will be able to tell you all about the class of car they own, and most likely the complete history of the car they brought to the track. The end result is that a spectator at a vintage racing event gets to see the old open wheel racers from before World War II, the English and Italian racers of the 1950s, the high-powered Ferraris, Jaguars, Cobras and Corvettes of the 1960s, and, at some events, some of the recent Can-Am and Formula 1 cars that may have raced only overseas. It all adds up to an impressive race weekend.

Chapter 1

On the Starting Grid

As one vintage car race driver says, "The most important piece of safety equipment is between the back of the seat and the steering wheel." Common sense plays a big part in safety at vintage races. The drivers are aware of the importance of the machinery entrusted to them on the track and the part that they play relative to the car. According to long-time vintage racer David Love, "The car has already made its history. There are no more records that can be written by the people who drive these cars today. It's already in the books."

With those words in mind, it's interesting to note the procedures that are in place to be sure the drivers don't get carried away with the competitive aspects of a race and damage the cars. In vintage racing, driver safety and the preservation of priceless racing cars are, or should be, foremost in everyone's mind.

In most events, if a driver shows a dangerous attitude on the track, he or she is asked to leave. Anyone who dents or damages their own or someone else's car while on the track is through racing for the year. No appeal. In a different sanctioning organization, the driver damaging a

Shelby Mustangs versus Cobras versus Corvettes—that's what sports car racing was about in the 1960s. A 1966 Shelby Mustang GT350 289 ci leads a 1965 Shelby Mustang 289 ci, a 1962 289 Cobra and a 1963 Corvette 350 ci during a Modified Sports and GT car race at Palm Springs.

car is out for the current race and goes on probation for a year. Another incident during that year and you're out for good. In this sport, a small mistake can have disastrous results. You're racing, but you're not racing at 10/10ths.

Each of the vintage events carries its own liability insurance, but the cars are not covered while they are racing. There is no insurance available for a vintage car while it is on the track, and this is incentive enough for the owners and drivers to exercise prudence when the racing gets excessively competitive.

Still, in recent years the driving has become more competitive. As more and more drivers get on the same track with someone like Stirling Moss, they try to prove they can go head-to-head against a known name. The amateurs at times end up driving over their heads, and damage and injury can result.

Another challenge to track safety is that some of the drivers and owners may not possess skills to match the cars they're driving. Referring to the Ford GT40s at the reunion held in 1989 at Watkins Glen, Carroll Smith, the manager of Shelby-American's Ford GT40 racing team in the 1960s, observed: "These automobiles were capable of killing the finest race drivers in the world twenty years ago. Today they're being driven by doctors and dentists!" Remember that the GT40 was capable of 220 mph. Fortunately, at the GT40 reunion cool heads prevailed, and no car or driver was involved in any accidents.

Technical inspections are the first item of business when a race car arrives at the track. Inspectors are looking for safety related details, fluid leaks, problems with wheels and tires, and originality of components. The tires are a major concern to the inspectors, as the original sizes and types of tires for many of the older race cars are no longer available. When similar kinds and sizes are found, they may have a stronger adhesion factor that puts additional stress on the car's suspension and wheels.

The tech inspectors are people who have previous experience with a variety of vintage cars. Within a group of inspectors, someone will have specific knowledge of each type of car. A master book, outlining the original configurations for each car that's been raced in that area, is usually kept on hand by sponsoring organizations.

Adding roll bars and other safety equipment to older cars that didn't originally race with them is opposed to by most owners. These attachments to frames that weren't designed for them can adversely affect the handling of the cars as well as grossly change the car's appearance. Most organizing groups have recognized the owners' concerns, and the older cars are running without roll bars. But internal fire extinguishers for the cockpit and engine, fuel cells and safety clothing for the drivers are common requirements. And the newer full-face helmets and Nomex fire-proof clothing are a far cry from the goggles and leather jackets of yesteryear.

The drivers get a briefing from race officials on what is expected from them on the course before taking to the track at Road Atlanta. The personal safety of the drivers and preservation of the vintage cars is a high priority at all vintage events.

Two tech inspectors check David Love's 1958 Ferrari 250 Testa Rossa's engine for oil leaks or any other problems that might disrupt the races or be a hazard on the track. The red valve covers on the Ferrari are where the name Testa Rossa (redhead) came from.

The preparation of 1960 and 1961 Ferrari 250 SWB Berlinettas at the Monterey Historical Races in California. This was a dual-purpose Ferrari as some were bought to race and many were bought as street cars. With a weight of 2,500 pounds and power of 280 hp, the car was capable of 150 mph. These two racers are well-used by World Ferrari of Long Lake, Minnesota.

A beautifully refurbished and race-equipped 1962 MGA 1800 cc belonging to Curtis Jones gets a tech inspection at the Atlanta Historic Races at Road Atlanta.

Checking the 5.5 liter engine of a 1932
Studebaker Indy for worn or leaking parts
is one of the many areas that are
scrutinized by the tech inspectors prior to
the car getting a safety sticker that allows it
on the track. The inspectors need to be
familiar with many different cars, and a
master manual helps to check the
specifications on those cars that are rare or
don't often race.

Formula cars get ready in the pre-grid area at northern California's Sears Point Raceway near San Francisco. The drivers wear the latest in protective safety clothing; here driver John Buddenbaum adjusts the Nomex head gear which is protection from fire and is worn with a full-face helmet.

Chapter 2

Vintage Racing Automobiles

One hears the terms vintage and historical used in different ways around these events. If you're talking to someone from England, the term vintage means cars constructed prior to World War II; historical cars are those built after the war. In the United States the terms are used differently within the many organizations that oversee each race.

Racing groups and classes

The many organizations that sponsor and sanction vintage car races don't completely agree about how to organize the groups and classes that will share the track at any one event. Many times other factors—such as the number of cars entered, the overall performance of a particular car or the level of competence of the driver—will determine the class that a car races in on a particular weekend.

Many major vintage events divide the cars into racing groups based on the type of car, year of manufacture and engine displacement. The cars are then further subdivided into classes within the groups for racing purposes.

A surprisingly nimble 1911 Fiat S74 GP driven by George Wingard rounds the Corkscrew at Laguna Seca Raceway in southern California. The Fiat's engine displacement is double the size of a 427 ci Ford Cobra engine. The car was the first of three brought to the United States in 1911 and run by Caleb Bragg in the races at Savannah, where he took fourth. In 1912, Bragg won the American Grand Prix that was held in Milwaukee, Wisconsin. Wingard acquired the S74 complete and in nearly original condition, making restoration easier.

The groups presented here are general and reflect the average breakdown of car classes.

Pre-World War II

By today's standards, automotive technology was primitive for cars manufactured before World War II. Some cars even had a hand-operated oil pump; the driver had to periodically pump up the pressure or face an engine failure. Still, many of these old cars with monster engines are capable of speeds up to 90 mph.

Within this group you might see the following kinds of cars: Bugatti, Maserati, BMW, Jaguar SS, Alvis, Lancia Kappa and Lambda, Ford-Rajo and Model T, Chevrolet, Morgan, Aston Martin, Austin, Buick Speedster, Stutz, Alfa Romeo, MG, Amilcar, Bentley, Vale, Peerless, Fiat, Delage, Studebaker Indy, Essex, and Lagonda. You may never have heard of some of these names, but others read like a history book of the automobile. They're all out there and they run—maybe even better than when they were new.

Vintage and Historic Production Sports Cars

These are high-volume production sports cars such as the Austin-Healey, MG, Alfa Romeo, Jaguar, Aston Martin, Lotus and Porsche. They are evenly matched, with close racing and speeds in excess of 140 mph. Most spectators can relate to these cars and may even have had a street version of an MG or Spitfire back in the 1960s.

At the upper end, and sometimes referred to as historic, are the race-prepared sports cars like the Corvette, Shelby Mustang, Jaguar E-Type, Lotus Elan and others built from 1960 through 1968. The owners must retain the original size engine and wheels, and the cars must not be modified beyond what the factory provided as optional equipment in the year the car was produced.

A number of cars in the Vintage Production Sports group are still actively racing in Sports Car Club of America (SCCA) club events. You'll still find MGs, Triumphs, Corvettes, Cobras and Mustangs in the twenty- to thirty-year-old age bracket racing for points one weekend and leisurely strutting their stuff at a vintage event a week later. This is a testimonial to the longevity of the cars and the continued entertainment they have provided.

Vintage and Historic Sports Racing

Sports racing cars were built specifically for racing, but have to conform to the class requirements: each car must have two seats, wheels covered by fenders, doors, lights and a horn. In the past, many of these cars were driven to the track, raced and then, with luck, driven home. Some of the notable manufacturers represented in this group are Ferrari, Porsche, Lotus, Elva and Lola. Cars of the historic period of sports racing were produced from the 1960s to the early 1970s.

The later cars in this category include the Canadian-American Cup (Can-Am) racers. When you see the orange McLarens on the track, it brings back the days of Mark Donohue and Denny Hulme.

Formula

Open-wheeled Formula cars, including the Formula Junior class that began in 1957 and Formula 1 and 2 up to the year 1963, comprise this group. The Juniors are sometimes classified into separate categories for

1957–59 front-engined, 1957–59 rear-engined and 1960–63 rear-engined. The group includes vehicles manufactured by such names as Vanwall, Cooper and Maserati. As they run the circuit, they bring back memories of Fangio, Clark and Hill.

Exhibition

The Exhibition group has a less competitive atmosphere. At some races Exhibition drivers are allowed to pass only on straight sections and when the slower driver acknowledges the pass with a hand signal. The result is a fast touring event, but it does give some of the drivers a chance to experience the race course and the spectators to see some of the cars that the owners really don't want to subject to the rigors of racing.

Also included in the Exhibition category may be cars that don't qualify as historical or vintage. Most notable among them are the relatively recent Formula 1 cars that no longer race in competition, but are unique to the enthusiast who has seldom experienced these cars on American tracks. It's also an excuse for the owners and drivers to get in a few laps in some sophisticated machinery.

The huge 14 liter engine in the 1911 Fiat S74 GP has a single overhead camshaft, four valves for each of the four cylinders and dual ignition. Horsepower is estimated to be between 180 and 200; the engine uses regular gasoline. The car weighs 3,200 pounds and is excessively front-heavy. The Fiat S74 was the last of the large slow-turning, 2200 rpm engines; in 1913 the rules were changed to eliminate the large-displacement engines from competition and favor the smaller, high rpm engines.

The 1916 Chevrolet 490 racer driven by Court Whitlock at Laguna Seca. The first Chevrolet race car—call it the Corvette's great grandfather. This early Chevrolet racer has a 2800 cc engine.

The 1927 Bugatti Type 35 GP of Robert Seiffert at the Monterey Historical Races. Designed and built by Ettore Bugatti in France, the Type 35 was constructed from 1924 through 1931 and was responsible for over 1,500 victories during its production lifetime.

Typical of early cars is this steering-wheel-mounted ignition and throttle control. The throttle control was to set the idle speed of the engine and even worked like a crude cruise control when the car was under way. This is a rare 1927 Vauxhall Type 30/98 Velox four-seater Tourer.

An aluminum-bodied 1927 Vauxhall Type 30/98 Velox four-seater Tourer leads a 1937 Bentley 4 1/4 into Turn 1 at Lime Rock Raceway in Connecticut. This same Bentley raced at Watkins Glen in 1948, where it finished fourth overall. The car is part of the Collier Museum collection in Naples, Florida; note the addition of the oversized roll bar to protect the driver—and the car—in case of a crash.

The 1965 Jaguar E-Type 4.2 liter belonging to Howard Turner is typical of the 1960s production sports cars that are returning to the track for vintage racing. The E-Type inherited racing technology from the famous D-Type racing cars that preceded it; for example, the E-Type's front suspension was straight from the D-Type. The original E-Type had a 3.8 liter six-cylinder engine with the 4.2 liter six coming later. In 1971 a V–12 was fitted to the model.

*Bob Gregory's 1961 Ferrari 250 SWB
Berlinetta at speed on the back straight at
Sears Point Raceway. The car is a steel-
bodied street version of the 250 SWB
Berlinetta aluminum alloy-bodied
competition cars, and it spent its first 11
years in Switzerland before coming to the
United States.*

Previous page
This 1964 Sunbeam Tiger Le Mans coupe is one of two cars that were a factory effort at Le Mans in 1964; this car broke after nine hours of racing. The fiberglass fastback covers a huge gas tank necessary for Le Mans competition, and a speed of 162 mph was clocked down Le Mans' Mulsanne Straight. The following year the Tiger Le Mans was runner-up European National Champion against Brian Redman and the lightweight E-Type Jaguars. This Tiger Le Mans came to the United States in the 1970s but never raced here. Syd Silverman purchased the car and prepared it for vintage racing.

Located in the small engine bay of the 1964 Sunbeam Tiger Le Mans coupe is a large 260 ci V-8 Ford engine that was prepared in England using Shelby parts. The carburetion is from twin dual-downdraft Carters. The engine produces 270 hp, considerably more than the 164 hp that was standard in street Tigers.

A brace of Cobras at Sears Point Raceway charge around a corner in close formation. The Cobras, especially the 289s, are much more plentiful at West Coast vintage events than in the East. Leading the pack is number 97, a 1962 Cobra 289 driven by Lynn Park, with number 49, a 1963 Cobra 289 driven by John Hall, bringing up the rear.

Racing the concrete canyons of the Palm Springs Vintage Grand Prix, these production sports cars are led by a 1965 Alfa Romeo GTA of 1570 cc, followed by a 1952 Jaguar XK120 of 3442 cc and a 1966 Alfa Romeo GTA also of 1570 cc. Even though the concrete walls can be hard on racing machinery, it is necessary for crowd protection on street courses.

David McCarthy pilots a 1952 Jaguar C-Type down the back straight at Sears Point. The racing C-Types were capable of 140+ mph, with racing fuel consumption averaging 16 mpg. This is the type of efficient performance that took the C-Type to first place at Le Mans in 1951 and 1953. The car is powered by a 3442 cc double-overhead-cam six-cylinder engine putting out from 200 to 230 hp, depending on carburetion.

Duncan Emmons in the cockpit of his 1953 Allard J2X. An aluminum-skinned hot rod built in England by Sydney Allard with big American V–8s shoe-horned into them, these cars dominated club racing in the early 1950s. The cars went on to compete in the 24 Hours of Le Mans, where an Allard posted a third overall against much more sophisticated machinery.

Previous page

A shiny skinned 1956 Lotus 11 driven by Walter Thomason at Sears Point. A lightweight aluminum body set on a tubular frame added up to a light and fast car with even a small engine; this was the philosophy of the Lotus factory when they placed an 1100 cc engine into the 840 pound car. It was a Formula car with just enough body pieces to make a "sports car."

The mean-looking 1958 Lister-Corvette with Bill Cizar aboard at Laguna Seca. Carroll Shelby put Chevrolet small-block V-8 engines with up to 400 hp into the Lister bodies. Visibility was one of the problems with the car due to the high hood, and drivers often had a difficult time placing the cars into corners.

Briggs Cunningham took on the sports car racing world in the early 1950s by designing and building a series of race cars, the most successful of which was this 1952 C4R. The Cunningham race cars competed in both the United States and Europe, the ultimate goal being to win Le Mans. The C4R shown here was the Sebring winner in 1953 and came in third at Le Mans in 1954. The car is powered by a Chrysler Hemi V-8 of 5424 cc displacement with four carburetors, turning out 325 hp. This was a successful American designed, built, powered and driven effort.

Phil Hill and Olivier Gendebien won Le Mans in 1961 with this Ferrari TR61 that now belongs to Peter Sachs. The car was also driven by Innes Ireland, Stirling Moss and Pedro Rodriguez, giving Ferrari another World Championship in 1961. This was the last of the front-engined Testa Rossas and looks considerably different from the 1957 and 1958 early Scaglietti bodies with its refined air intake and aerodynamics.

This 1959 Ferrari 246S Dino with a V-6 2.4 liter engine was one of four cars built by the factory. It took second place at the Targa Florio with Phil Hill driving. In 1961 it was rebodied with a high tail. The V-6 was good on the short courses but wasn't competitive in long distance races. The car is now campaigned in vintage racing by Kendall Merritt.

A 1962 Lotus 23–B rounds a corner at Road Atlanta with Donald Brooks driving. The Lotus 23 is essentially a Lotus Formula Junior with full-width bodywork and a 1600 cc engine.

Dan Gurney winds down the Corkscrew at Laguna Seca during the 1989 Monterey Historical Races in a 1958 Vanwall Formula 1 car. Number 2 is one of only two cars of this type to come to the United States, and it ran for the first time here at the 1989 Monterey Historics. The Vanwalls won the World Constructors Cup Championship in 1958.

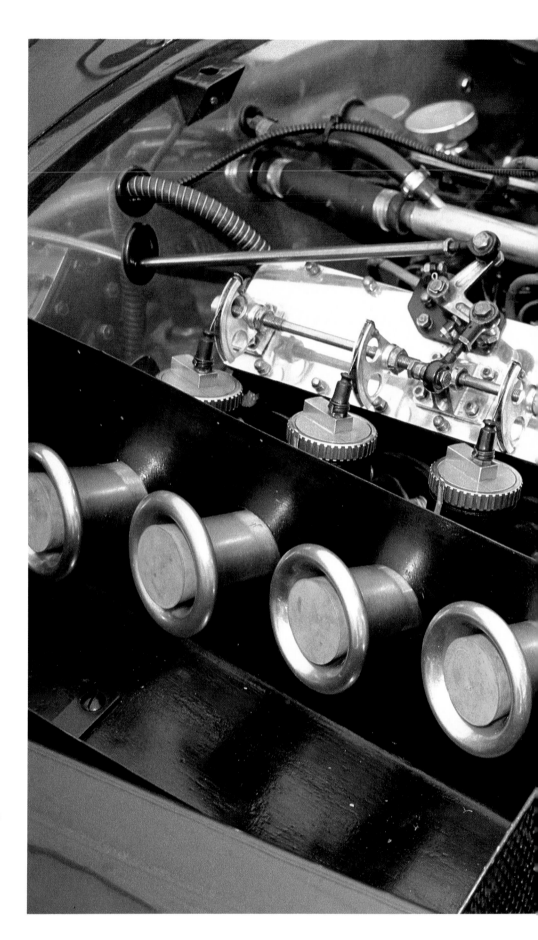

The powerplant for the Vanwall Formula 1 car was designed after the Norton motorcycle engine. It was a 2.5 liter four-cylinder twin-cam aluminum-block engine, with four valves and two spark plugs per cylinder. Fuel delivery came from mechanical fuel injection.

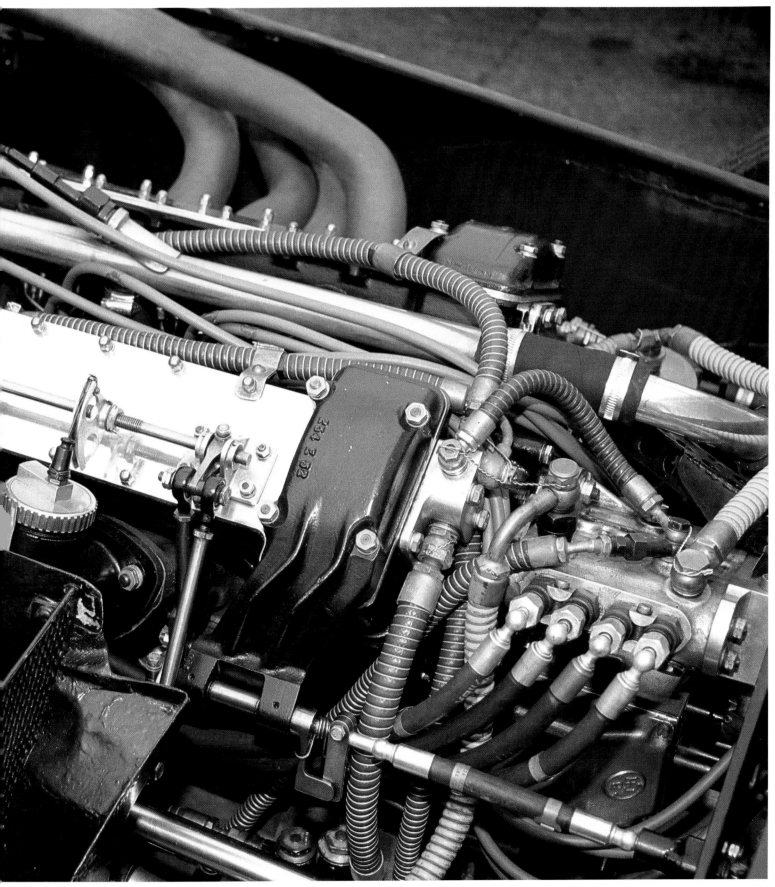

Previous page
A 1959 Elva Formula Junior driven by John Bloch. The Formula Junior class was derived to give drivers a chance to develop their skills before moving up to the faster, more sophisticated cars. Starting in 1957 the first Formula Juniors started to appear with strict rules pertaining to weight and engine type and size. England joined the Formula Junior fray in 1959 with the Elva being one of the more competitive entries.

George Raterink in his Italian 1959 Stanguellini Formula Junior, a car that dominated its ranks in 1959 due to its superb Fiat-based engine. In 1960 Formula Junior became a proving ground for Formula 1, and in 1963 Formula Junior was changed to Formula 2 and 3.

A 1959 Gemini MK2 Formula Junior built in England by Checkered Flag Racing and raced by famed driver Jim Clark prior to his tenure with Lotus. This was the first single-seat race car driven by Clark. The car is shown here being driven by Lou Canut at Laguna Seca.

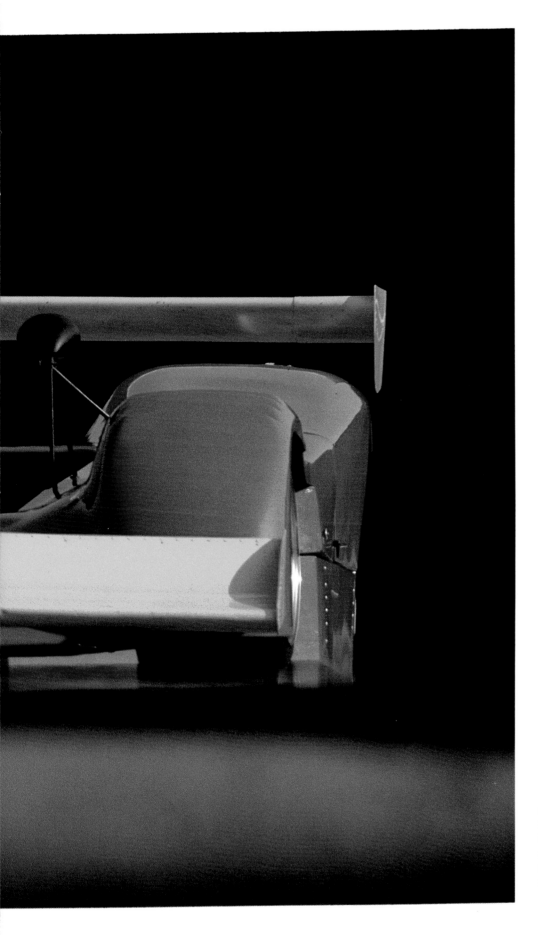

A car devoid of the usual sponsor signs is this 1973 Lola T-330 Can-Am racer. On the borderline of vintage eligibility, this automotive sculpture pleases enthusiasts at any track where it performs. The Lola is shown here with owner Steve Rees at Turn 7 of the Road Atlanta course.

Previous page
A 1970 Porsche 908/03 with Ernst Schuster dives through the famed Corkscrew at Laguna Seca. The compact 908/03 was designed to take the place of Porsche's 917 at the Targa Florio and Nurburgring endurance races, which the cars promptly won.

The V–12 Westlake engine of the 1972 Gulf Mirage M6/603 driven by Toby Bean and Brian Goelnict in the Watkins Glen Vintage Cup Aston Enduro.

The 1974 McLaren Formula 1 car powered by a 3000 cc engine and driven by Bill Perrone doesn't qualify for vintage status yet but is raced along with other relatively recent Formula 1 cars in the Exhibition class. With most of the Formula 1 action taking place in Europe, it is a rare treat to witness and hear this type of race car. As quickly as Formula 1 racing changes, these cars become historical (non-competitive) in a relatively short time.

Chapter 3

Restoration of Vintage Racers

How many times have we heard the one about the valuable vintage sports car found under a tarp in some farmer's barn in Kansas or Montana? It surely has happened, but today the salted-away treasures are harder to find. Most of the older Jaguars and Cobras have been found, restored and brought back to life. Now it's the more exotic and rare cars that are coming to light, and some of these new old cars are coming from even more exotic locales, such as South America and Mexico.

The fact that many old cars are finally being resurrected is not a factor of new technology. Escalating value is bringing in old cars that previously were too expensive to restore. People who have stored away a race car from another era are looking out in the shed and realizing that what they have under that tarp is now valuable.

One car's history: 1924 Delage 2LCV V-12

Designed in 1922 by Charles Planchon for Louis Delage and built in 1924 in the form of four Grand Prix race cars with eight to ten engines, the Delage 2LCV was a landmark car in the history of motor racing. This race car had the first V-12 engine built to fit a specific racing formula: two liters, unsupercharged. Raced in the 1924 French Grand Prix held on the Lyons circuit, the Delages came in second and third behind an Alfa Romeo.

After the 1924 season, this car was bought by a wealthy Anglo-Argentine, Juan Malcolm, to be raced in Argentina's 1927 Rafaela race. The

Previous page
The fully restored 1924 Delage 2LCV makes its debut at the 1989 Monterey Historic Races with owner Bob Sutherland at the wheel. This is an excellent example of the resurrection of an important piece of

automotive history by a vintage race car enthusiast. The project started in 1977 and took 12 years, much research and quite a few dollars before the restored Delage saw the track.

Two Delages corner during the 1924 French Grand Prix. The two cars finished second and third behind an Alfa Romeo. This corner, complete with grown trees, still exists near Lyons, France. Geoffrey Goddard Collection

The Delage V-12 engine during its restoration with the complete geartrain laid out. The gears turned the four shafts of the double overhead cams, the two magnetos, and the oil and water pumps. Two of the gears shown here had to be made from scratch while several others were reconstructed from the old damaged pieces. In total, 450 individual parts were handcrafted for the engine. Steele Therkleson

car and a large quantity of spare parts were shipped off to Argentina.

With Malcolm driving, the car won the Rafaela 500 and several other races during 1927. Another Argentine race driver, Cesar Millone, then purchased the car, but his record with the car is undocumented. Next, a Frenchman named Estanguet took possession, and in 1929 or 1930 rolled the car in a race, damaging it badly.

Several owners later, the car was in the hands of Fernando Verisco, who may have run it in a speed trial in 1934 or 1935. The history books place a Delage at a 1942 race in the town of Mendoza on the opposite side of the Andes Mountains, only 200 miles from the city of Santiago, Chile, where the car was rediscovered in 1973 or 1974 by a local Honda dealer. He realized that the Delage was probably an important car in the history of motor racing, but he knew that no one in Chile could afford to take on the job of proper restoration, so he decided to sell it to someone in the United States.

The car was advertised in *Hemming's Motor News* with only a small picture of the engine. Vintage car enthusiast Bob Sutherland recognized it, however, and had it shipped to the United States. When the car arrived in 1977, restoration looked like a hopeless task. The chassis parts were shipped on to England while the engine stayed at the shop of Steele Therkleson in the Los Angeles area.

The engine had arrived loosely bolted together. Therkleson took it apart and for the next year assessed the problems of restoration and researched how the engine worked. Little information existed about the car, much less the mechanics of the V-12 engine—no valve timing, no firing order, nothing. To complicate matters further, the parts had come from at least four different engines, evidenced by mismatched part numbers.

Therkleson made the engine roller bearings from scratch and

rebuilt or remanufactured other damaged parts; a total of 450 individual parts for the engine alone were handcrafted without drawings. Eight years of painstaking research and labor were necessary before the engine rumbled to life outside Therkleson's shop.

The chassis was rebuilt at Bassett Down Engineering in England, and Duncan Rickets re-formed the body from photographs that had been taken on glass plates in 1924. These photographs were the only reference for other parts that had to be made from scratch, including the steering box, brakes and radiator. Only sixty percent of the original Delage engine and about forty percent of the chassis parts were recovered; all of the body

and the rest of the engine and chassis were completely reconstructed by artisan mechanics.

The finished engine was shipped to England, where it was reunited with the restored chassis and body. The Delage was then shipped back to the United States to make its debut at the 1989 Monterey Historic Races at Laguna Seca in southern California.

The culmination of the Delage project will come when Sutherland and Therkleson take the car back to France and drive it around the same streets that made up the 1927 Lyons Grand Prix circuit.

Reconstructing bodywork

What does a vintage race car owner do when a body panel is

The two-liter V–12 Delage engine assembled, but with the front of the timing case removed to show the geartrain, the double overhead cams and three of the six spark plugs on one bank. This was the first V–12 engine to be built to conform to a specific racing formula. Steele Therkleson

missing or damaged? You can be sure none will be available at the local dealer or auto graveyard. The part must be rebuilt from a blank sheet of metal. Not many craftsmen are still proficient in the hand skills that can hammer, bend, roll and shape metal to form a perfect Cobra or Ferrari fender. When you consider that the original Cobras were built individually by artisans in a small shop, it's only

This photo, taken in 1924 at the Delage factory on an 8x10 in. glass plate, offered much of the details needed to finish the Delage's accurate restoration. The photograph was originally printed in several magazines during that era. The picture shows the meticulous engine turning painstakingly added to the engine and bodywork. This circular pattern put onto the metal parts was found even on the inside of the body parts. Geoffrey Goddard Collection

proper that a body piece be replaced in the same manner.

Body craftsmen are predominantly from Europe, where the time-consuming hand skills still survive. This is a craft acquired only through long years of apprenticed labor.

Many shops are specialized in the work they perform. One will do bodywork, some wheels, another painting and another exclusively upholstery. But a few large shops do have the knowledge to do the whole car, from bodywork to seat covers.

The worst scenario is when an irreplaceable car is wrecked and burned, then neglected. If the old frame and engine can be resurrected, body parts can be replaced, and the car can be made to run again. This is one of the reasons that an owner can—with only a little trepidation—put a million-dollar car at risk on a racetrack. Short of total destruction, the car will be fixable at a cost considerably less than the value of the car.

Rebuilding engines

As with the Delage, restoring a one-of-a-kind engine can be complex, timely and expensive, and the artisan mechanics capable of this level of work are difficult to find.

In the process of rebuilding some of the old engines, the choice can be made to improve a few internal flaws that might cause failure on the track. This minor re-engineering is accepted in most circles, but modifications that increase power and torque beyond what was legal and available when the car was first raced are not allowed. At times, a fine line can separate the two.

Some vintage racers run engines in their cars that are still being manufactured; others may be available in junkyards. These engines are of course easier and less expensive to race and rebuild.

Over-restoration

In recent years some restorers have gone to such great extremes that

everything on the car is made perfect. Some people in vintage racing circles look on such restorations as over-doing it as the original car just wasn't that perfect. The consensus is that race cars should be restored only to the point that they were when they were new. But on the other hand, a race car is never finished. During its racing period it will undergo numerous modifications and be in a constant state of evolution and development. The owner can pick any one of the past configurations for restoration, but one representing the car at its zenith is preferred.

A company reconditioning a valuable car may try to improve the symmetry, fit of the panels and paint of a car, if for no other reason than that the restorer's reputation is on the line. Bringing a car back to its original shabby state could be misconstrued as

poor work by the restoration shop. Thus many of the cars being reborn today are actually back in better than original condition.

1958 Ferrari 250 Testa Rossa

David Love has campaigned the 1958 2953 cc V-12 Testa Rossa for twenty-six years, from the time it was an SCCA contender in D Modified, now called A Sports Racing over two liters. The Testa Rossa raced against obsolete Can-Am cars, modified Cobras and anything with an American V-8 motor in it.

Love originally paid $4,500 for the car in terrible condition. The car had been crashed at Laguna Seca, ending upside down in a tree at old Turn 4. A previous owner had partially restored the car and Love bought it unseen. The continued restoration was an extended project as

Rolled out on the grass at Bassett Downs in Wiltshire, England, the restored chassis of the 1924 Delage race car was complete except for engine and bodywork. Only forty percent of the chassis were available from the original car; all of the bodywork had to be reconstructed from photographs. Recent information has been uncovered indicating that more parts from the original car have been found in Santiago, Chile. Bob Sutherland

more information about the car became known.

Today, the car is virtually priceless. Because of his early entry into racing with the car, even before it was considered vintage racing, Love has been able to enjoy and nurture a truly significant automobile.

The cars are definitely the stars of vintage car racing, but it's the people

who make it happen and reap the ultimate enjoyment of the events. Reveling at any weekend are the patron owners that keep the museum pieces alive; the individuals that maintain a single show piece (whether it be Ferrari or Austin-Healey); the officials that organize, discipline and provide the safety factor; and, around the course, the spectators that come to remember, relive or find out what the history of the automobile is all about.

Colin Kimmins and an assistant work at Kimmins Coach Craft in California on a Beverly Shear to trim pieces of sheet metal to be formed to fit a C-Type Jaguar that is being restored. Around them are newly formed parts for a Shelby Cobra restoration. The old, thin and worn out metal sections of the car are used for patterns to make the replacement parts.

Colin and Bruce Kimmins use the English Wheel roller to shape a sheet of metal. The wheel actually stretches and displaces the metal to give it shape. This is the way body parts have been formed by hand for decades.

Cleco pins hold the bodywork together as Colin Kimmins hammers out high spots on the fender of the aluminum-bodied C-Type Jaguar. The pins temporarily hold the lower panels to the bodywork until permanent rivets are put in place.

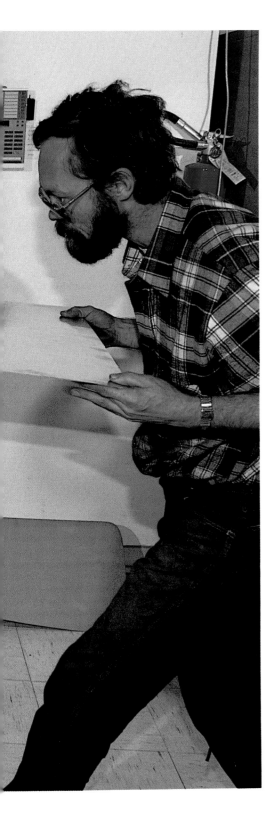

The 1958 Ferrari 250 Testa Rossa of
David Love leads the number 66 1959
Maserati Tipo 61 Birdcage of Robert Baker
at Laguna Seca. These two cars were the
last of an era of successful front-engined
race cars. Starting in 1961, both Ferrari
and Maserati were forced to switch to rear-
engined cars.

David Love at the wheel of the 1958
Ferrari 250 Testa Rossa in SCCA racing at
Laguna Seca in 1965. As more information
became available to him on the original
250 TR specifications, Love continued to
restore the car to its original condition.
David Love

David Love's 1958 Ferrari 250 Testa Rossa racing in SCCA competition in 1967 at Cotati, California. Several years later in the early 1970s this car and a few others came back to the Cotati track to start what is today vintage racing. After sweeping up the glass from the Saturday night drag races and putting out hay bales, the pioneer vintage racers first ran their cars around the track one at a time and later worked up to racing in groups. David Love

The 1958 Ferrari 250 Testa Rossa after Jack Graham crashed it at Laguna Seca in 1960. The car ended upside down in a tree. Two owners had the car after the crash before David Love took possession and completed the restoration. David Love

Next page
David Love's 1958 Ferrari 250 Testa Rossa is one of the 19 original Scaglietti-bodied cars. The engine is a V–12, 60 degree, single-overhead-cam unit that puts out about 300 hp. The 250 Testa Rossa was to be one of the most successful of all the front-engined Ferrari racers.

Chapter 4

Owners, Drivers and Enthusiasts

Owners and drivers

Not all the owners drive their own cars. Some have vintage racers that demand a high level of driving skill; in that case, a professional driver is often employed. Other owners bring several cars to the event and share the driving with friends of professional drivers. But most owners are also drivers, for being able to drive a vintage racer is the main reason for owning and restoring the car.

Patrons of vintage racing

Scattered around the paddock area at a vintage race several large trailer transport rigs with graphics on the side herald specific race teams or marques. These aren't professional racing teams that normally shuttle between professional events, even though they are better equipped than some that do. These are the transports of the patrons of vintage racing that have taken it upon themselves to keep alive many of the cars that would otherwise be relegated to storage or museums.

They often come with several cars, paid "wrenches" wearing uniforms or overalls, and often drivers with names like Moss, Innes Ireland and Dan Gurney to properly chauffeur the priceless machinery. They do it because they love the automobiles

Drivers in Sports Racing cars wait at the pre-grid for the chance to get on the Lime Rock track. A question mark in the future of vintage is whether the owners of these cars will continue to race them as their values skyrocket. The escalating price of production race cars is also starting to limit the number of persons at what used to be an entry level for new racers. Even Austin-Healey Sprites are getting expensive.

they bring, because they get to relive the ultimate racing moments in person, because it increases the investment value of these and other vintage cars and because they have a great time and can afford to do it.

Peter and Judy Giddings' Alfa Romeo and Maserati

Not to be classed with the high-dollar patrons are the car owners like Peter and Judy Giddings of Walnut Creek, California. They own several significant cars, including a 1932 Alfa Romeo Monza and a 1956 Maserati 250F Grand Prix racer. Peter trailers the car that he's chosen to drive on a particular weekend, and he and Judy do all the maintenance on the car.

It's a labor of love for the Giddings, with incredible effort placed on maintaining the authenticity of the cars. Details such as paint, engine and running gear have been thoroughly researched and maintained as closely as is possible to the original specifications.

Women on the track

Men aren't the only ones on the track with an appreciation for fine machinery and a desire to go fast. Journalist and professional driver Denise McCluggage raced in the original Formula Libre race at Lime Rock in July 1959. She returned with her pink polka-dotted helmet in 1989 in a Porsche RSK to duel again with the likes of Moss, Rodger Ward and John Fitch.

At other vintage events women were present in the cockpits of cars like the 1947 Bentley Special of Jennifer Lawrence, the 1962 Morris Mini of Patsy Bolling, the 1925 Lancia Lambda of Madelyn Guttman, the 1961 Austin-Healey Sprite of

Karyn White, the 1956 Lotus 11LM of Barbara Blackie and the 1960 Lotus 18 Formula Junior of Judy Morton.

MG Irish Racing Team

In the early days of SCCA club racing, the group of MG drivers that showed up at many of the same races were competitive with each other yet knew each other as friends. Today the MG Irish Racing Team is a similar group that shows up at East Coast vintage events and shares a camaraderie as well as knowledge and tools. The cars are relatively inexpensive, and some are still driven to the track. Socializing is as important as racing to the owners and drivers.

One 1954 MG TF was brought to numerous vintage races over a three-year period and never finished a single race weekend. The engine usually went during one of the qualifying races. *This* is dedication. The driver, Tom Finn, finally did it at Lime Rock and when he returned to the paddock after the last race, you would have thought he'd just won Le Mans. His jubilant friends gathered around him and his car, and the smile on his face said it all—just running and having a good time with friends is what it's all about.

Scott Renner's low-budget racer

The ultimate low-budget vintage racer is Scott Renner. Racing with a 1960 Austin-Healey bugeye Sprite, Renner drives the car to each track from his home in Venice, California, near Los Angeles. With an extra engine in the passenger's seat, toolbox, cans, clothes, sleeping bag, oil, straight pipe to replace the street muffler, jack and jack stand crammed in every nook and cranny of the diminutive

Dan Gurney gets a briefing on the 1958 Vanwall Formula 1. Gurney is an example of the name drivers that originally drove many of the cars that are now back on the track enjoying a second life. Stirling Moss, John Fitch, Bob Bondurant, Innes Ireland, George Follmer, Rodger Ward and Denise McCluggage are a few of the other drivers who participate in vintage events and add their own history to the celebration.

Stirling Moss at the wheel of a Maserati 250F Formula 1 car. This is the same type of car that Moss and Fangio were successful in during the 1956 and 1957 Grand Prix seasons, winning the World Championship in 1957.

The cockpit of the Maserati 250F is stark compared to today's race cars. The three main information sources were the tachometer, water temperature gauge and oil pressure gauge, all visible between the spokes of the huge wooden steering wheel.

Sprite, Renner goes vintage racing. The extra engine is to make sure he can still drive home if he bends the existing powerplant.

Using an extra-large car cover as a tent, he sleeps in a sleeping bag next to the car in the paddock area. For about $24 in food, gas, oil and the race entry fee he probably has as much fun as the Ferrari driver that came with his car in a transport and will sleep in the best of hotels. He manages to race at many of the regional races, and also ran at Road Atlanta in 1988. The true enthusiast is as important to vintage racing as the owners and drivers with the high-dollar mounts.

Track volunteers

You don't have to own a vintage car to be part of the action. It takes many dedicated enthusiasts to carry off a weekend vintage event. The people registering the participants and press, tech inspectors, track stewards, corner workers and safety crews are all necessary to make it happen. Some have aspirations to own a vintage racer, others are spouses of racers or other workers, while most are friends who meet at vintage events. The one thing they do have in common is a keen interest in the cars on the track and the safety of the drivers.

Jerry Etzel looks as though he is about to be eaten by his 1959 Austin-Healey Sprite. Etzel has prepared it exactly like the Sprite that Moss drove for the factory in 1960 at Sebring. It's a replica of that configuration done with lots of research and luck in finding the right parts. Etzel is a mechanical engineer and does this for relaxation alongside three or four owners of similar cars. Together, they prepare their cars for the race.

Ed Archer looks the part of a vintage racer with his 1915 Ford Model T derivative. He brought the car 120 miles to the Monterey Historical Races in the back of a 1924 Chevrolet one-ton truck.

Next page
Peter Giddings with the 1932 Alfa Romeo Monza at Laguna Seca. This car was once the South American champion, driven by Baron Manuel de Teffe. When recently raced at La Carrera in Mexico, it won its class and averaged almost 100 mph, beating dozens of far newer cars, the fastest enduro race average attributed to this type of Alfa Romeo. Although the car has a great value today, Giddings believes that cars are moving sculptures that should be viewed by an appreciative public.

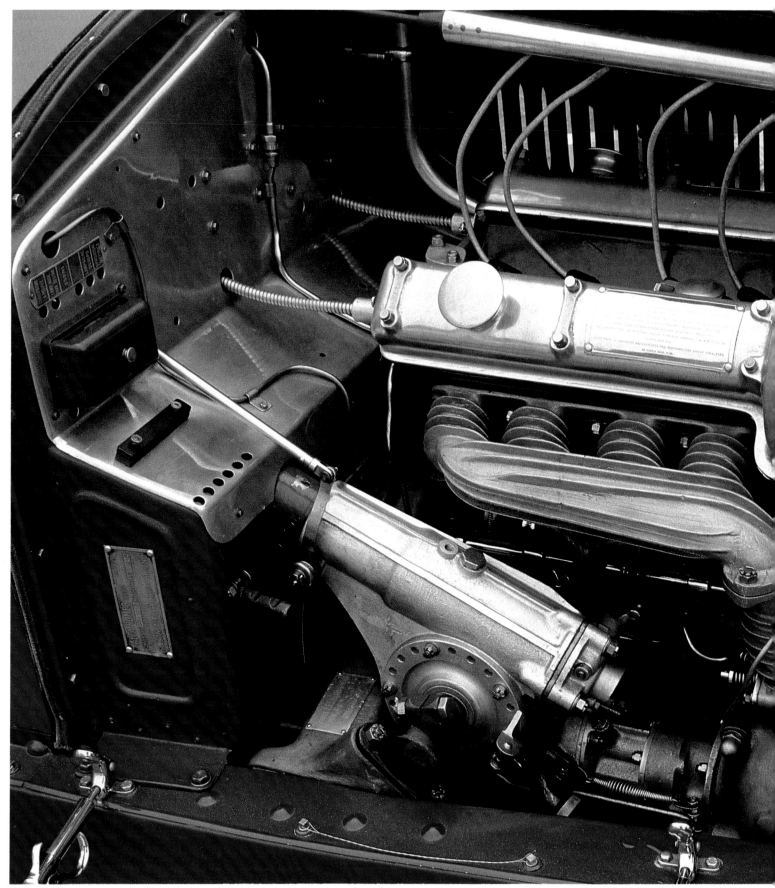

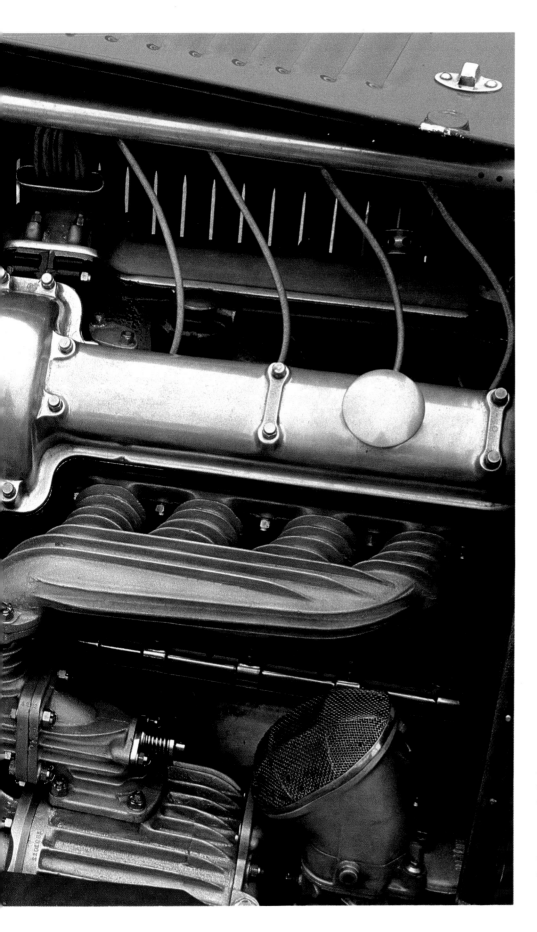

The 2300 cc engine of the 1932 Alfa Romeo Monza was designed by Vittorio Jano, using a single carburetor in front of a supercharger to produce 180 hp. The eight-cylinder engine makes extensive use of ribbing on the intake manifold to cool the air and gas mixture before it gets to the engine, similar to today's intercooled turbo engines. Depending on the drive ratio fitted to Alfa Romeo, it was capable of speeds up to 140 mph in 1932.

Merit Shalett from New Orleans gets ready to enter the Watkins Glen track with her Lotus 23. At the GT40 twenty-fifth anniversary reunion, Shalett shared the track with the GT40s in Group 5 and raced against them in the two-hour enduro.

Next page
Karyn White in her 1961 Austin-Healey Sprite that originally raced with a three-woman team in 1961 that included former Indy race driver Janet Guthrie and Denise McCluggage. The team and the car raced at places like Le Mans and Sebring, and during this time the car was painted pink. Not many women are actually involved in the driving of race cars at vintage events. At the 1989 Monterey Historical Races, only five of the 316 entrants were women.

Denise McCluggage in a 1959 Porsche RSK re-creating her role in the 1959 Formula Libre event at Lime Rock. Note her pink polka-dotted helmet, her trademark over the years.

Members of the MG Irish Racing Team in the paddock at Lime Rock, complete with banner, British flag and a number of vintage MGs. The red car in the foreground is a 1950 MG TD. Meeting at vintage events in the northeast, they come from Long Island, Bridgehampton, Lime Rock and Pittsburgh. The usual procedure is to get as many races out of an engine before it goes and then wait until the next season. This is called low-budget and no-budget racing.

Scott Renner, the ultimate low-budget racing enthusiast, prepares his 1960 948 cc Austin-Healey bugeye Sprite for competition. Note the extra engine in the passenger's seat. If the installed engine quits, Renner can either part-out the extra engine or install it, making it possible to continue racing and, more importantly, get back home.

The red 1966 Alfa Romeo GTA of Ron and Fred Cziska gets a workover between races. GTAs race with MGBs, Lotus 7s and Morgans to name a few. The Production Sports car group is evenly matched and usually produces some close racing.

A thumbs up and the checkered flag are the sought-after rewards for the vintage car racer. No purse money is involved in vintage racing. It has been said that the car owners take their trophies home on their trailers.

The 4.4 liter six-cylinder engine in William Ziering's 1955 Ferrari 121 LM unexpectedly quits just before Turn 6 at Laguna Seca. Car and driver will receive the dreaded and humiliating tow back to the paddock area.

Chapter 5

Reliving History: Special Events

Enduro races

Enduros have names like the 24 Hours of Le Mans, 12 Hours of Sebring, Daytona and Targa Florio. Many of the vintage cars racing today are enduro cars that were specially designed to go fast and do it for a long time. Vintage racing enduros don't last as long as the races they emulate—they range from ninety minutes to three hours—but they do tax the machinery in the same way and add the element of strategy made necessary by required pit stops and driver changes. A set number of pit stops of specific length with strict rules for refueling and repairs are factored in with the highest mileage at the end of the time limit.

Enduros aren't the most entertaining form of vintage racing because the faster cars soon lap the slower ones, and it's difficult to follow which car still has a pit stop to accomplish. The winner may not even know he or she is the winner until the time is up and the official results are posted. The spectators must satisfy themselves with watching the goings on in the pits and just enjoy the wide variety of race cars at speed.

From the driver's standpoint, enduro racing is different from the sprint around the track to get in front of the next competitor. Here the driver must go as fast as possible without

The most famous GT40 of them all, the Mark I that won Le Mans in 1968 with Pedro Rodriguez and Lucien Bianchi, and 1969 with Jacky Ickx and Jacky Oliver. It also won races at Watkins Glen, Brands Hatch, Spa and Sebring. Gulf placed the car on display at Indy, and in 1984 it became the property of Harley Cluxton.

putting undue stress on the car—a conflict of terms if there ever was one because if it breaks, you're done. The amount and type of traffic during an enduro also keeps drivers alert. The slower cars are constantly being descended upon and the big boys are using the slower cars as pylons to weave in, out and around.

Marque races

At each vintage race a manufacturer that has left its mark on automobile racing is usually honored. The marque is given a prominent place in the weekend's activities, such as a parade lap for those in attendance or a special race to place a large number of that car on the track at one time.

Steve Earle's Monterey Historic Races are probably the best example of honoring a given marque. Ford, Ferrari, Maserati and Aston Martin are only a few of the marques highlighted at the Laguna Seca course. Every conceivable example of that car is likely to appear. The factory brings cars, owners bring cars, famous drivers show up and, as in the case of Aston Martin with the Le Mans pits, illustrious history is re-created for all to enjoy.

At the smaller races the honored marque gives the owners of those cars an added incentive to gather with others having like machinery. The end result is a grand reunion and a great cross section of any one make. Such was the twenty-fifth anniversary gathering of Ford GT40s at Watkins Glen, New York, in 1989.

Re-creation races

A gathering of the main players in historical car racing events has

become a way to re-create the excitement of past spectacles. Two great re-creations in 1989 brought some great cars and drivers together for the enjoyment of both participants and spectators.

At the XVI Monterey Historic Automobile Races held in August, Aston Martin re-created the Le Mans pits from 1959, when its cars won the race and, subsequently, the Sports Car Championship. Aston Martin brought the winning DBR1 race car as well as three other DBR1s—four of the five cars that ran in the race. As the honored marque at the 1989 Monterey Historic Races, Aston Martin also rolled out two DBR2s, three DBR2Ss and one of the DP Project cars.

Re-creations aren't complete without the people who made the original event. Here, too, Aston Martin had great representation at the 1989 Monterey Races: Sir David Brown, who owned Aston Martin in 1959; Ted Cutting, who designed the Le Mans-winning car; and Gillian Harris Stillwell, the former team secretary. And what about the drivers? The six who together won the 1959 Sports Car Championship—Stirling Moss/Jack Friedman, Roy Salvadori/Carroll Shelby and Paul Frere/Maurice Trintignant—were on hand to reminisce and talk with the multitude of enthusiasts.

Another re-creation, this time of the race itself, was the Formula Libre

Next page
The gathering at the Glen brings 38 GT40s to the racetrack for a 25th Anniversary reunion. Nearly a third of all the GT40s built (134 chassis) attended the reunion, with 16 running in the Exhibition race.

Drivers line up at the pre-grid for a GT40 Exhibition race at the 1989 Watkins Glen Serengeti Vintage Cup. These GT40s became a hallmark in automotive history when the United States showed the established European road racing manufacturers that American auto makers could compete on an even or better level with Detroit V-8s and racing technology.

event first held on July 25, 1959, at Lime Rock. Thirty years later on the same course many of the original cars and drivers assembled to re-create what was a very controversial race.

Sports car aficionados of the 1950s didn't give much credibility to the American midget race cars that were circling dirt tracks, and you can imagine the snickers when the Formula Libre race was set up

between five United States Auto Club (USAC) road-racing midgets, one Formula 1 car, two Formula 2 cars and twelve sports cars. This was the strangest mix of race cars to ever share a track.

The drivers of the midgets were no slouches. They included 1959 Indy winner Rodger Ward, National Champion Tony Bettenhausen and USAC's former director of competition, Duane Carter. The sports car contingent was well represented by Chuck Daigh in a Maserati 250F Formula 1 car, George Constantine in a 4.2 liter Aston Martin DBR2, Lance Reventlow in a Formula 2 Cooper, Dick Thompson in the futuristic Chevrolet Stingray, John Fitch in a Cooper Monaco, a young Pedro Rodriquez in a 300S Maserati and journalist Denise McCluggage in a

The four versions of the GT40. The Mark I, number 6, that started with Ford's Indianapolis engine, with later Mark Is receiving the 289 and 302 powerplants. The Mark II, number 3, first appeared in 1965 on a similar chassis to the Mark I but with the 427 engine. Seven Mark IIIs were built, shown here in dark blue, and designed for street use; the car shown here was originally presented to John Wyer by Ford. The Mark IV, number 1, was called the J car after a new regulation known as appendix J. The Mark IVs only raced in two events, the 1967 Sebring and Le Mans, both of which they won.

Porsche RS-550, to name a few.

The winner? Rodger Ward in the eleven-year-old Offenhauser-powered midget drove circles around the sports car types. Ward even decimated the outright Lime Rock track record

during practice—all this on the sports cars' own turf.

Thirty years later, most of the same cars and nearly all of the original drivers reassembled back at Lime Rock to restage the famous Formula Libre race. For a few laps Ward again led the same cars and drivers—déjà vu. To protect an irreplaceable engine, Ward brought the midget in early and left the dicing to the sporty cars at his heels. There was nothing to prove; all that had been done thirty years previously.

Once again a re-creation had brought together friends that hadn't seen each other in decades, presented a glimpse of an exciting bit of history to the racing public and a wonderful time was had by all.

Concours d'elegance

Concours d'elegance events are beauty contests for cars, and often include a class for vintage race cars. Prizes are awarded for best paint, best chassis, best in show and similar achievements. The most important aspect in judging the concours is how well the car is restored to its original condition. The judges painstakingly check each part of the car to be sure that it works. The engine, brakes, lights, turn signals and brake lights must all be functional in the original configuration.

Associated with the concours events are all the dinner parties and teas that make these a social occasion as well as an automotive display. Some of the concours are directly affiliated with a weekend's vintage racing.

The parade lap being led by 1968 GT40 Mark I number 6, the two-time winner of Le Mans. Number 6 is owned by Harley Cluxton and driven here by Brian Redman at Watkins Glen. The yellow number 1 GT40 Mark IV in the front row is George Stauffer in J-4, which won the 1967 12 hours of Sebring.

The Ford GT40 Mark IIs were fitted with
427 ci engines and used a beefed up chassis
that was similar to the Mark I's sheet-steel
tub. With 485 hp on tap, the Mark IIs could
hit a top speed of 211 mph.

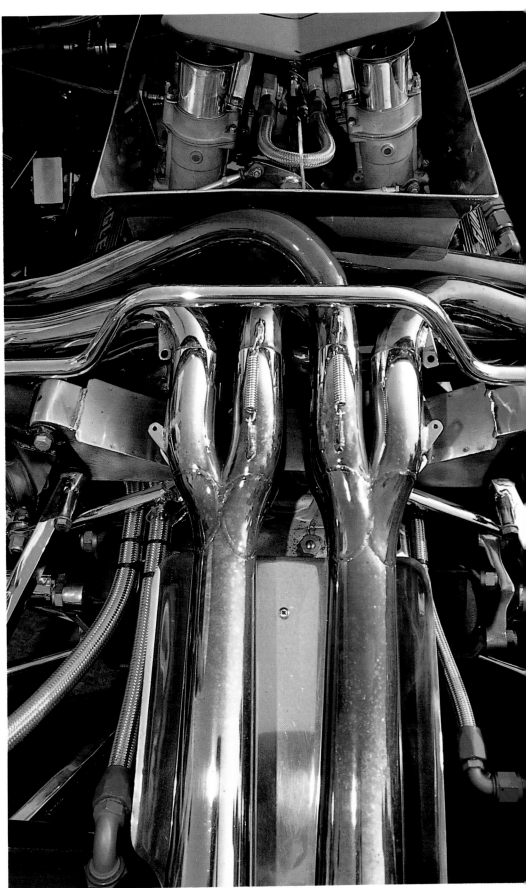

The 302 engine (the limit for the five-liter class) in GT40 Mark I number 7 with special Gurney-Westlake heads. This combination produced over 400 hp, propelling the car to 205 mph.

Last-minute adjustments to Jim Ladwig's GT40 Mark I show the 289 ci engine with the transmission removed. This car was used by the MGM film studio as a camera car for the movie, Grand Prix. For many years the car was displayed at the Briggs Cunningham Museum.

The 1989 Laguna Seca Historic Automobile Races re-created the 1959 Le Mans Aston Martin pits in honor of the marque's thirtieth anniversary of their endurance race victory. The 3670 cc double-overhead-cam, twin-plug, in-line six-cylinder in the 1957 Aston Martin DBR2. Power in Le Mans tune was 287 hp at 5750 rpm.

The re-creation of the 1959 pits at Le Mans at the 1989 Laguna Seca Historic Automobile Races was the centerpiece for a weekend of vintage races that honored the Aston Martin marque and the thirtieth anniversary of their victory at Le Mans. In front of the Le Mans pit replica are the Aston Martin DBR1s, DBR2s, DB2s and a DP Project car.

The winning drivers and celebrities from the 1959 Aston Martin team meet the enthusiasts in front of the re-created Le Mans pits at the 1989 Monterey Historical Races. In the midst of the fans are Sir David Brown, Jack Fairman, Paul Frere, Stirling Moss, Roy Salvadori, Carroll Shelby and Maurice Trintignant—nearly all the important players from the 1959 Le Mans victory.

The DBR2 cockpit with wood-rimmed steering wheel and full instrumentation. Moss drove this car, DBR2/2, in December 1959 to a win at the Bahamas Speed Week at Nassau, the last time Aston Martin ran an open-cockpit car in a sports car race.

The 1959 Le Mans winning team of Carroll Shelby and Roy Salvadori takes a lap at Laguna Seca at the 1989 Monterey Historic Automobile Races. Shelby retired from racing in 1960 and went on to Cobra fame. Salvadori continued with Aston Martin, finishing his career with a victory at Monza in 1963.

Paced by Rodger Ward in his midget and Moss in the Maserati 250F, the field is ready to start the re-creation of the 1959 Formula Libre race at Lime Rock in 1989. Ward once again led the sports car field for several laps until his engine started to fail.

Rodger Ward in the Kenny Brenn midget leads the Aston Martin DBR2 driven by Rex Woodgate (taking the place of George Constantine, who was in the original race 30 years ago). Note Ward using the brake handle on the outside of the car. When Ward won the race in 1959, the Kenny Brenn midget was already 11 years old.

How to Photograph a Vintage Race

With a little bit of planning and a 35 mm still or video camera, you can bring some of the memories of a vintage race back intact. Those of you who have sophisticated camera systems with zoom and telephoto lenses can combine two hobbies into one encounter and come away from a vintage race with photographs to grace a wall or win a contest.

I've put together a few tips used by serious racing photographers that may not only help to give you better pictures, but also add a lot to how well you see the action of a race weekend.

Equipment
Cameras

Even though a basic point-and-shoot camera can give reasonable pictures of the overall track situation and close-ups in the paddock, the best camera system for race photography is the 35 mm single-lens-reflex (SLR) camera, preferably of the type that allows interchanging lenses. On the track you'll want telephoto capabilities and in the paddock a wide-angle or close-up lens will allow you to capture details of the vintage cars. For the serious photographer, a motor drive or winder and autofocus will help to get even better results.

Lenses

Zoom lenses and long telephoto lenses will give you the versatility and means to frame your subjects when you may not be able to change your position in relation to the race cars on the track. The zoom lenses I prefer are in the 28 to 80 mm range for general photography in the paddock and 80 to 300 mm for shooting on the side of the track. Many photographers already have an 80 to 200 mm or 70 to 210 mm zoom, so you may already

be set for many picture-taking situations.

The addition of a long lens in the 300 to 500 mm focal lengths will help to visually compress the cars as they come toward you, or will allow a large subject in the frame in those areas where you must stay back from the track.

Teleconverters of 1.4X and 2X power can be combined with some lenses to increase their focal length. Remember that they lose light and can degrade image quality to a degree— the most noticeable loss is when a 2X converter is used in conjunction with a zoom lens. And be aware that the longer the lens, the harder it is to follow-focus a moving car.

Autofocus is another tool that can add to the percentage of sharp photographs. Standard autofocus is useful for cars that are passing parallel to the photographer, but not if the car is coming directly toward the camera. The delay between the time the focus is sensed, the shutter button pushed and the actual picture taken is long enough for the car to have traveled a number of feet and out of the original focus area.

Some of the newer autofocus cameras have what is called predictory or tracking autofocus. These cameras will predict by computer how fast the subject is moving and place the focus in front of the subject so it is at the right spot at the moment of exposure. With this type of camera system you can get sharp photographs even when the car speeds directly at the camera.

Film

Finer grain films in the slower ISO range are best. For slides, I recommend Kodachrome 64,

Ektachrome 100+, and Fujichrome 50 and 100. If prints are your preference, the color negative films from 25 to 200 ISO are the best bets when it comes to making an enlargement later.

Just bring plenty of film. You can easily use five rolls of thirty-six-exposure film during a day of racing, and I've been known to shoot more than fifteen rolls a day when seriously covering a race.

Taking photographs
On the track

Start the day by getting a program, giving you the layout of the track, a listing of the cars and drivers, a schedule of events and usually a number of interesting facts about the history of the more important cars.

Wander around the track early. Make a point of checking each of the corners for shooting angles, and note from which direction the light is coming and will be coming as the day progresses; one corner can be great in the morning and horrible later in the day. The best light will hit the front of the car and shine on the side that you're photographing. The light direction may be less critical on days that are overcast.

Look for fast sweeping corners that will have cars leaning into their suspensions. This can be emphasized from a low angle. I also look for hills and rises where the car can be isolated against a neutral out-of-focus background. On the other hand, sometimes a sign or logo in the background will add to a photograph.

Another section of the track to look for is an area for panning with the cars. Be sure the light is coming from your side of the cars and onto the front of them. Choose a combination of shutter speed and f/stop that will give you a blurred background and a sharp car. Start with a shutter speed of 1/250 second and progress down to 1/60 second. The percentage of sharp cars will diminish with the slower shutter speeds, but the effect will be more dramatic. The idea is to frame the speeding car before it passes you and follow it as it sweeps past. Time your release of the shutter just prior to the car's being in front of your position, and be sure to maintain a good follow-through. The outcome depends on how well you match the speed of the car with your pan.

Remember that the success of these techniques requires lots of tries, hoping you get one that is just right. Don't count your shots until you see them in a finished print or projected on the screen.

In the paddock

At some point during the day, spend some time in the paddock area. Here you can get close to the cars, see the details, and talk to the owners and drivers. A wide-angle to normal lens can capture some of the flavor of the festivities, while a close-focusing lens can get the camera in tight to photograph the details of wheels, badges and engines.

The medium telephoto zoom (70 to 210 mm) can also help to get that portrait of the celebrity driver. A shot of Moss, Gurney, Carroll Shelby or Bob Bondurant would fill out the group of photos on the wall. Use the telephoto end of the zoom focal length and fill the frame with the head and shoulders of the person—up close and personal.

The finished results can be one large blockbuster print on the wall, a grouping of smaller prints that tell the overall story of the race or a slide show for friends that is refreshingly short and leaves them wishing for more.

Photographs in this book

All of the author's photographs in this book were taken with Canon EOS cameras, primarily the EOS 630 and EOS-1. Lenses were Canon autofocus, which included 24 mm, 28 to 80 mm zoom, 100 to 300 mm zoom, and the 300 mm f/2.8 with 1.4X (420 mm) and 2X (600 mm) autofocus teleconverters.

Film for all the images was Fujichrome 50 and 100. On normal sunlit days the 50 ISO film was used extensively. When the weather became overcast or long lenses were to be used, 100 ISO film was used.

Vintage Racing Organizations

AARA
Antique Auto Racing Association
PO Box 343
Columbiana, OH 44408

ACOT
Atlantic Coast Old Timers
55 Hilliard Road
Old Bridge, NJ 08857

AHRMA
American Historic Racing Motorcycle
Association
Route 2, Box 214
Marento, OH 43334

ASRA
Arizona Sports Racing Association
4446 E Shomi Street
Phoenix, AZ 85044

CARE
Classic Automobile Racing Enthusiasts
3010 SW 14th Place, Unit 12-13
Boynton Beach, FL 33435

CARS
Classic Auto Racing Society
1321 Beryl Street, #306
Redondo Beach, CA 90277

CHR
Chicago Historic Races
825 W Erie Street
Chicago, IL 60622

CSRG
Classic Sports Racing Group
PO Box 488
Los Altos, CA 94022

CVAR
Corinthian Vintage Auto Racing
PO Box 232
Addison, TX 75001

DAARA
Daytona Antique Auto Racing
Association
705 Lost Tree Trail
New Smyrna Beach, FL 32069

DVVGP
Delaware Valley Vintage Grand Prix
Association
303 #6 Willow Grove Avenue
Philadelphia, PA 19118

Greatrace, Ltd.
9304 Forest Lane, Suite 200-A
Dallas, TX 75243

Highlands Classic
PO Box 1652
Highlands, NC 28741

HMSA
Historic Motor Sports Association
PO Box 30628
Santa Barbara, CA 93130

HRG
Historic Racing Group
PO Box 84852-75257
San Diego, CA 92138

MBHR
Meadow Brook Historic Races
4140 S Lapeer Road
Pontiac, MI 48057

MVP
Mountain View Promotions
PO Box 3704
Littleton, CO 80161

NLRC
Nelson Ledges Road Course
3709 Valcamp Road
Warren, OH 44484

NDRA
Nostalgia Drag Racing Association
PO Box 9438
Anaheim, CA 92812-7438

PVGPA
Pittsburgh Vintage Grand Prix
PO Box 2243
Pittsburgh, PA 15230

PSVGP
Palm Springs Vintage Grand Prix, Inc.
330 E Sunny Dunes Road
Palm Springs, CA 92264

RMVR
Rocky Mountain Vintage Racing
61 Golden Eagle Lane
Littleton, CO 80127

SCCA
Sports Car Club of America
9033 E Easter Place
Englewood, CO 80112

SDAM
San Diego Automotive Museum
PO Box 127088
San Diego, CA 92112-7088

SOVREN
Society of Vintage Racing Enthusiasts
PO Box 3816
Federal Way, WA 98063

SVRA
Sportscar Vintage Racing Association
2725 W 5th North Street
Summerville, SC 29483

USCRA
United States Classic Racing Association
RFD 3 Box 441
Richmond, NH 03470

VARA
Vintage Auto Racing Association
3426 Knoll Drive
Los Angeles, CA 90068

VARAC
Vintage Auto Racing Association of
Canada
3300 Yonge Street, Suite 202
Toronto, Ontario, Canada M4N 2L6

VFCA
Vintage Formula Car Association
1129 Monserate Avenue
Chula Vista, CA 92011

VMR
Vintage Motorcar Racing
1800 Market Street #20
San Francisco, CA 94102

VR
Vintage Racing
PO Box 7000-728
Redondo Beach, CA 90277

VRCBC
Vintage Racing Club of British Columbia
Box 23393
Vancouver AMF, BC, Canada V7B 1W1

VSCCA
Vintage Sports Car Club of America
116 Long Ridge Road
Bedford, NY 10506

VSCDA
Vintage Sports Car Drivers Association
Box C, 15 W Burton Place
Chicago, IL 60610

VSCR
Vintage Sports Car Racing, Inc.
9403 Union Terrace
Maple Grove, MN 55369

WHRR
Waterford Hills Road Racing, Inc.
c/o Oakland County Sportsman's Club
4770 Waterford Road
Clarkston, MI 48016

WMCVG
Walter Mitty Challenge Vintage Group
PO Box 550372
Atlanta, GA 30355-2874

WGOT
Williams Grove Old Timers
1 Speedway Place
Mechanicsburg, PA 17055

The 1963 Lotus 27 with Joel Finn aboard takes a victory lap around the Lime Rock track after winning the 1989 Kendall Cup. The Lotus 27 won the English and European Formula Junior titles in 1963— the last year that Formula Junior was run.